Self-Image Demystified

The Proven Art of Attracting What You Want by Becoming What You Want

(without trying so hard)

Law of Attraction Short Reads, Book 8

By Elena G. Rivers

Copyright Elena G. Rivers © 2021

All rights reserved. No part of this publication may be reproduced, stored in a retrieval system, or transmitted, in any form or by any means, electronic, mechanical, photocopying, recording, or otherwise, without the author and the publishers' prior written permission.

The scanning, uploading, and distribution of this book via the Internet or any other means without the author's permission are illegal and punishable by law. Please purchase only authorized electronic editions and do not participate in or encourage electronic piracy of copyrighted materials.

Elena G. Rivers © Copyright 2021 - All rights reserved.

ISBN: 978-1-80095-069-6

Legal Notice:

This book is copyright protected—it for personal use only.

Disclaimer Notice:

Please note the information contained in this book is for inspirational and entertainment purposes only. Every attempt has been made to provide accurate, up to date, and completely reliable information. No warranties of any kind are expressed or implied. Readers acknowledge that the author is not engaging in the rendering of legal, financial, health, medical, or professional advice. By reading this book, the reader agrees that under no circumstances are we responsible for any losses, direct or indirect, which are incurred as a result of the use of the information contained within this book, including, but not limited to, errors, omissions, or inaccuracies.

The information provided in this book is for entertainment purposes only. If you are struggling with serious problems, including chronic illness, mental instability, or legal issues, please consult with your local registered health care or legal professional as soon as possible. This book is not a substitute for professional or legal advice.

Contents

Introduction - 8
The Art of Changing Yourself Without Changing Yourself 8

Chapter 1- 17
The Science of Becoming a Truly New Person 17

Chapter 2 - 37
Release Your Old Programs and Stop Fighting Yourself (The Art of Manifesting from a Place of Neutrality) 37

Chapter 3 - 43
When Being Driven or Motivated May Turn Against You (The Hidden Dangers of Self-Improvement) 43

Chapter 4 - 56
How to Create Your New Joyful Habits & Aligned Discipline (and the One Crucial Thing Most People Miss) 56

Chapter 5 - 67
Why Your New-Self Image Wants to Test You (and When Negative Outcomes Are Not Really That Negative) 67

Chapter 6 - 73
When Abundance Doesn't Follow Confidence 73

Chapter 7 - 84

The Simple Mindset Shift Behind Unstoppable Motivation 84

Chapter 8 - 94

Creating Your Own Unique Process to Manifest Desired Results 94

Chapter 9 - 99

Hidden Obstacles to Avoid (and the Real Truth about FOMO) 99

Chapter 10 - 104

Amplify Your Self-Image with Powerful Thoughts (What Most Gurus Don't Want You to Know) .. 104

Conclusion – Trust Yourself 109

Join Our Manifestation Newsletter and Get a Free eBook 111

More Books by Elena G.Rivers 113

Introduction - The Art of Changing Yourself Without Changing Yourself

I used to believe that changing my self-image was about trying hard to acquire better social skills or attempting to look more confident so that everyone around me would see my new power and approve of me.

I used to believe that changing my self-image was about acting: pretending and forcing myself to be someone else to manifest my dreams, and then I would eventually feel good about myself.

And, lastly, I used to believe that if I saw someone else succeed and I copied them, behaving and doing things precisely as they did, then I would finally be successful.

Unfortunately, this way of thinking led me on a somewhat misaligned journey for several years. Years of trying hard to be someone I wasn't so that I could manifest something that, first of all, wasn't for me, but also wasn't making me happy, and wasn't even my true goal.

The Art of Changing Yourself without Changing Yourself

But now, looking back, I'm grateful for my journey because I learned from my mistakes. My old triggers are now my healers, and it's thanks to my journey, I feel authentically confident to write this book and hopefully uplift and inspire you on your journey too!

You see, I see this pattern all the time, especially in the self-development community. "I want to change myself; I want to improve myself."

Don't get me wrong; I'm all for self-improvement and learning - I'm on this journey too. It's never-ending and genuinely fascinating. Since I discovered the power of authentic self-image, my self-development and spiritual journey got much better and more effective. I get better and quicker results with less time spent on "trying to improve myself" or "trying to learn more."

I used to try hard to improve myself because deep inside, I thought I wasn't good enough. I used to think to myself, "When I finally discover that one thing, that one secret, or that one method, then I will be able to transform myself and attract all my desires."

(By the way, back then, I didn't really know what my true desires were, so I tried hard to manifest other people's goals and desires so that they would approve of me and I could finally feel better about myself).

But here's the most considerable truth I discovered: changing your self-image is not that much about changing it or trying hard to being someone else. It's all about getting to your roots and your authenticity. It's about embracing who you are without trying hard to conceal your imperfections or seeking validation or approval. It's about being grateful for every little step you take on your journey and loving yourself just the way you are.

It's about embracing the fact that you are already good enough and don't have to improve anything. Instead, you can allow yourself to take action from a place of curiosity and mindful exploration.

For example, when you buy a new book, pay for a self-development or spirituality program, undertake professional training (business, marketing, etc.), or make any other investment in developing your skills, what you learn will be so much more effective if you truly understand this:

The Art of Changing Yourself without Changing Yourself

You are good just the way you are. You don't have to change anything. Instead, focus on mindful and joyful exploration from a place of curiosity and authenticity.

This is the exact approach we're taking in this book. As far as I'm concerned, it's supposed to be a fun and joyful experience. We don't want to experience any resistance while we're going through this process.

At the same time, sometimes, you may experience some negative feelings of self-guilt or self-blame.

For example, many people may start experiencing thoughts such as, "Why did I waste so much time chasing after something that wasn't really my goal? Or, why didn't I think of all this earlier? It would have saved me years of needless effort and frustration!"

And yes, as I said, I have been there too; I used to be the Queen of Self-Guilt Trips. But here's one thing to understand - we constantly change; our emotions, mindsets, and energies are always evolving. And we always do the best we can, with what we have available. So, don't worry about what would have happened if you had only known about specific techniques earlier on your journey.

The Art of Changing Yourself without Changing Yourself

Instead, choose to be grateful. The way I see everything now is that *we don't fail: we succeed, or we learn*. So, everything that you experienced on your journey so far got you to this very moment. Even negative experiences can make you stronger if you allow them to shape you into a stronger person.

So, if you ever experience any negative or self-defeating thoughts while reading a self-help book (even a book that is meant to be positive and uplifting, like this one), allow yourself to stay in this feeling from a place of neutrality. Just let it be.

And then, thank it for guiding you. Just say, *"Thank you for letting me know and reminding me that my journey is essential. Also, thank you for protecting me for so long. But now, I choose to move on and let go. It's all about learning, and nobody is perfect."*

To give you an example, I recently had a conversation with someone in the Law of Attraction (LOA) community. He is a pretty well-established thought leader in the spirituality space, with several best-selling programs that he offers and thousands of successful students. Despite all his success, he told me that he felt like completely changing one of his programs because he

The Art of Changing Yourself without Changing Yourself

felt like he was wrong, and therefore felt bad for sharing his message with so many people.

I asked, "So, why do you think you were wrong? I think your programs are excellent. I had many 'aha' moments as I was going through them, and so did many others."

And he said, "Oh yeah, but I feel like other teachers might be doing it better because they get more followers, and because of that, people automatically assume that their way is better. And that thought made me realize that perhaps I didn't make the right decision with my course; when I first created it, I didn't know what I know now."

I told him, "Look, different people resonate with different content and philosophies. As soon as you focus on who you indeed are and what you believe in and create from a place of authenticity and alignment, you will attract people who think and feel similar. Just like you're already doing!

And of course, as a teacher, you are also a student, and you always learn and expand. Today you know and understand more than you did several years ago. You can choose to be content because you are growing and

The Art of Changing Yourself without Changing Yourself

evolving, or you can choose to beat yourself up because, five years ago, your content wasn't as good as it is now."

Please bear in mind, my dear reader, that the above story can be applied to pretty much everything in life, not just business or creative endeavors.

And, when you get on the journey of exploring your self-image and working on your mindset and energy, you, too, may get caught up in some negative, self-blaming thoughts. Of course, I'm not saying this to be negative, and I'm not saying this will definitely happen to you. From my observation, I'd say it does happen to many people, even the leaders and teachers in the self-development and spirituality space.

So once again, remember that we all do the best we can with what we have. It's not about perfection; it's about progress.

When you are grounded in who you truly are, manifesting your dream reality becomes almost automatic, and you don't need to worry about what to do because your actions are aligned with your thoughts and feelings. You know what your desires are. You feel whole and complete, even before your dreams come true. In fact, you are already living a dream, and it's only getting better and better!

It's time to create your own life philosophy and live accordingly. It's time to design your own life mission that makes you excited to get out of bed in the morning. It's time to stop comparing yourself to others too!

Success is all about knowing who you are and what you want. It's not about chasing other people's goals or trying to pretend you're someone else (been there, done that, and it didn't work).

Finally, knowing your own definition of success, based on your authentic self-image, will help you create your own manifestation process. Attracting basic and simple things daily, without resistance, leads to miraculous manifestations. And you can't lose, because, with this system, you either succeed or learn!

It's time to get back on your unique life path while mindfully designing your philosophy, mission, and process.

Oh, and if this is the first time you're reading my work, even though this book is a part of *the Law of Attraction Short Reads* series, it stands alone. You don't need to read any of my other works to understand my approach to self-image, manifestation, and the Law of Attraction.

Like most of my books, this book is also written as a practical, step-by-step system. However, it is not my intention to indoctrinate the reader into any specific way of thinking or acting. So, even though I think this book is more effective if followed step-by-step and read several times, I want you to use your own judgment and intuition. My intention behind writing this book (and all of my books, really) is to assist my readers and give them the tools they can use to create their own transformation systems. After all, we are all different! So, as you go through this short book, feel free to take what you like and reject the rest.

My mission is to help raise the vibration of the planet by helping people help themselves and others. It all starts with you. I hope this little book will provide you with at least one helpful idea or tool you can use to manifest your dream reality. However, don't forget you are already living in one, and it's only getting better and better!

Chapter 1-The Science of Becoming a Truly New Person

True, aligned identity shifting is our biggest friend on this journey. This is how we can create a permanent mindset and energy shifts that help us become the next version of ourselves to reach new levels of success and fulfillment on our journeys.

Anything you see in the physical world and desire to attract into your life requires an internal shift. And both must be aligned.

Yes, you can achieve or attract something by pure luck. For example, a person may win or inherit a large sum of money. But since their internal world may not be fully aligned with it, they may sabotage their luck and lose it all.

Another mistake that people make is that they think they want something, and they change their inner world and try hard to attract it. However, in the process, they become someone they are not meant to be (as I already shared in my intro), and they manifest a reality that doesn't make them as happy as they thought it would (yes, I've been there too). Then, it takes even more work and effort to get back to their old identity or desperately to try to find something else.

Your external world reflects your internal world, which is fantastic news because it means that we genuinely get to shape our reality.

Unfortunately, most people just blindly want to shift their identity without understanding what they want. For example, I spent several years thinking I wanted to become a famous influencer with a big online presence, offering expensive packages, simply because I saw other people do it. I didn't dive deep enough into my inner wisdom and intuition to figure out what I wanted to do with my life. At the same time, I was stuck in wanting, and since the goal I put on the pedestal wasn't for me anyway, I always found it extremely hard to take action. As a result, what I could have tested in three months would take me more than three years.

Luckily, I finally woke up and re-connected with my genuine desire to be a writer. Everything became much easier for me. Not only that, but I could also finally put my energy into something that had the potential to help and inspire people all over the world.

The Science of Becoming a Truly New Person

Knowing your actual goals is so crucial. But don't be hard on yourself if it takes a while to figure it out. The process of figuring it out and mindfully testing out different options can also be fun. It can also help you become a proactive person who never gives up, loves researching different options and testing them without getting too attached to the end result! In other words, becoming your own detective to figure out your goals and desires can be a goal and a journey in itself. If you are one of the seekers who still feel bad because they don't know their vision or purpose yet, don't worry. Just become a detective for now and enjoy this experience!

Then aside from knowing what you want and what your actual goals and desires are, you must get clear on who you need to become to attract them. In other words, you need to align your inner world with what you would like to appear in your physical world. Your new self-image will be the bridge in this particular operation!

When I say, "You need to get clear on who you want to become," please note that it will be getting back to being the younger and more authentic version of yourself in some cases. The passionate person you were before you got distracted by trying to become someone you were not meant to be and ended up in a burnout.

Ask yourself, what would it feel like to experience stretching your current comfort zone without resistance to living your dream reality? What are the small baby steps you can take now to start experiencing your dream reality? For me, for example, it's to carry on writing this book. While my old self likes to pop in occasionally and tell me to scroll on Facebook, I'm still here writing. I understand that it helps me expand my comfort zone and align myself with my new self-image.

You need to be someone who can feel authentically confident to start doing new things, think new thoughts, and holistically be a new person. There are several steps you can take, even before you're done reading this book.

Your environment (physical and social) matters.

I used to be in a negative environment where people were complacent and not supportive of my goals. But I was passionate about self-development and learning more about the Law of Attraction. For a long time, I felt terrible about myself, and I even thought there was something wrong with me because my old friends would just laugh at me. I remember talking about books like 'Think and Grow Rich' and hearing ridiculous comments such as, "OK, all right, I'm gonna tell my boss that from now on I want to get paid, just by thinking!" or books

The Science of Becoming a Truly New Person

such as '*How to Win Friends and Influence People*' and the comments I would hear went on like, "Haha, you need to read books on how to meet new friends! Haha, maybe instead of buying all those books, give me your money or buy me some drinks, and I will tell you how to make friends!"

That was many, many years ago, and I'm actually laughing now when I think about it. But back then, I felt very hurt because of all those comments, and for a long time, I felt torn. I felt scared of losing what I thought were my friends at that time, but at the same time, I wanted to explore self-development because a part of me felt I could improve my life and do something positive in this world.

So, to cut a long story short, I moved cities and used it as an excuse to stop seeing my friends. At the same time, I began meeting new friends, and all of them were into self-development. I could finally talk about all those excellent books I was reading, and since my new friends were into seminars, I felt happy that I could finally attend one of those too!

That simple experience taught me the importance of mindfully choosing my environment. Your results, ambitions, and energy are heavenly influenced by the people you surround yourself with. And the effect they have on you can be positive, negative, or neutral. But you can always choose a new circle of friends. Please note, I'm not saying you have to do what I did and leave your old friends behind, unless, of course, you consider them toxic and feel like you are no longer aligned with them in any way, and have nothing in common (which is what I felt).

Moving cities or countries can also be an option for those who can explore it. While such an option is not for everybody, it's definitely more of a high-water jump, as it forces you to adapt and become a different person, therefore, altering your self-image.

However, you can also choose to change your internal environment, even without leaving your old friends and surroundings behind.

Constantly changing places and friends can also become a negative pattern of escaping the old and chasing the new, and I have been there too. (That could be the topic for a memoir, now that I think of it, haha.)

The bottom line is: what consumes your thoughts, actions, and energy? Is that source positive and aligned with your new goals and desires, or is it negative and depriving you of your whole, creative potential?

To help you better understand this, I will briefly introduce you to the concept of pendulums, which is one of the main pillars of my favorite book: '*Reality Transurfing*' by the Russian writer and quantum physicist Vadim Zeland.

In his book, Vadim Zeland explores the concept of pendulums, which are invisible energy-informational structures that directly affect us in daily life and, in some cases, can even control how we act, feel and think.

There are positive and negative pendulums. Not all pendulums are bad. For example, let's say you want to manifest learning a new skill. You want to speak French fluently or play the piano. In alignment with your goal, you may go online and find some groups, courses, communities, and people with the same purpose or passion. In other words, you may join a positive pendulum of people who are on a similar journey and emanate equal energy that unifies them. You may even get invested in some classes or courses. This would be an example of a positive pendulum that helps you evolve into the person you need to become to get closer to your goals.

But there are also negative pendulums. An extreme example of a negative pendulum is war. Others may be a cult, gang, sect, or any environment with negative thought energy. Sometimes a negative pendulum may seem innocent at first and lure you in with something that seems optimistic. For example, as I was chasing the old "goals" that weren't even mine in my old life, I got seduced by many pendulums hiding as mentors, programs, and courses that were promising me instant fame, gratification, or abundance.

Negative pendulums know how to hook into your insecurities and lack of clarity, and they love feeding on your energy.

After reading Vadim Zeland's book, I decided to change my environment again and left several mastermind groups I was a part of at that time. I immediately felt a massive relief, as well as more clarity and energy. While the mastermind groups I left may have worked for others and their goals, they just weren't for me and my long-term fulfillment.

By the way, if you want to learn more about the concept of pendulums, I highly recommend Vadim's books!

The Science of Becoming a Truly New Person

However, understanding a small part is enough for us for now. Ask yourself:

- Am I under any negative influences now?

- Could it be that I'm doing something I think is positive, but that actually may not be suitable for me?

(Who knows, maybe you will even decide that I'm an evil pendulum and will choose to close this book and never talk to me again!)

Joking aside...

Give yourself some time and space to determine all the positive and negative influences in your life. Is there a way to eliminate or reduce the negative, or at least become immune to it for now?

Is there a way to increase the positive influences in your life? Whatever makes you feel good, inspired, and empowered.

How do you place yourself in your environment?

Can you mindfully use your new environment to speed up the creation of your new self-image?

An extreme example of this is moving to a new country and practically being forced to learn a new language, instead of trying to motivate yourself to learn a few new words here and there, without exposing yourself to the culture and language you wish to master.

Your appearance and habits also play a significant role in shaping your self-image.

For example, for years, I dreamed of being healthy and fit. I wanted to be healthy and fit, but my "wanting" would never go outside of the realm of wanting, needing, reading about different fad diets, and occasionally feeling jealous of or even judging people who had a healthy lifestyle and fit body. Eventually, I realized that my old self-image (someone who just wants and needs but never thinks, feels, and acts in alignment with their needs and desires) had to go.

I imagined and aligned myself with the healthy version of Elena. I asked myself if that person would sit on the couch, just wanting and reading about different diets, thinking she knows it all (with no actual results, but whatever!). I immediately felt like getting my hands dirty a bit and decided to go for a quick walk that even turned into a run. I felt so inspired and liberated. I got back home, had a shower, made a healthy, nutritious smoothie, and wrote in my journal, "I'm so happy and grateful that I'm finally free, and instead of learning more about how to lose weight and get healthier, I'm just doing it. I'm already feeling the first results!"

So, I kept thinking, feeling, and acting in alignment with my new self-image and began losing extra pounds without torturing myself with the latest fad diet. Just eating clean and wholesome food, most of the time.

(Yeah, I assumed that a healthy Elena can have a treat here and there and doesn't have to be a strict dieter because she's already in balance.)

Now, since I mentioned the importance of focusing on your appearance and making sure it's aligned with your new self-image, I feel like I need to expand on this. It may seem like I'm contradicting the message I shared in my earlier books, which is: it's not only about how you look.

So, to clear things up, I still stick to my old definition of "appearance." First of all, I'm not referring to trying to look different to please other people or impress others with the way you look or dress (unless it's your thing, or you are in a career where it's a part of a deal, or you are simply into fashion).

Your inner appearance and feelings come first. In my case, before losing weight, I saw myself as someone healthy and fit from the inside out, so I began taking action accordingly and manifested my first results. I no longer had to force myself to go for a walk or a short run. I just felt like doing it. Just like right now, I don't have to force myself to write. I simply wake up, have my coffee and start my day with writing.

I look forward to it because talking to you is always lots of fun (and by systemizing my thoughts and sharing my experiences, I learn a lot myself, so thank you for inspiring me!).

When I say 'appearance,' I'm referring to living a healthy lifestyle and taking care of your body, mind, and soul in general. As Jim Rohn says, *"Take care of your body. It's the only place you have to live."*

It's also about your lifestyle. If you are reading this, I assume you have great dreams and ambitions for your life, passion, career, or profession. Or perhaps you want to manifest more fun and freedom or quality family time. Whatever your goals and desires are (professional or personal), ask yourself if your current lifestyle aligns with what you desire. Are you already living in alignment with what you desire? Are you becoming what you desire? Your actions and choices are your best affirmations. And yes, in the beginning, there's often some resistance, which I totally understand. But taking that first step will make you feel so much better!

I remember that after I decided I wanted to become a writer, I began hanging out with many artists and creatives. I mistakenly assumed that this is what I needed to do to feel inspired. However, I soon realized that their choices, such as going out every night or complaining about "the pains of life," were not aligned with my goals of being a productive and positive writer who writes consistently and creates something that helps readers. (I'm not too sure if I could help you by writing books about how bad the world is and how hopeless we should feel, lol.)

Back then, I found myself partying and going out pretty much every night, and most people I hung out with were very talented people with lots of potential and many dreams, yet they would never take action. They were just out there in the clouds, complaining how difficult it was to make it out there as an artist or writer.

Now, I'm not judging because to each their own. Some people simply enjoy going out and having an active social life, and it aligns with their life goals of meeting new people or developing social confidence.

Also, I don't want to put labels on people. There are different kinds of creatives and artists, and not all of them are into partying. Some people may benefit from the inspiration they get when going out and talking to people. But the extreme nightlife and partying lifestyle weren't for me and weren't getting me closer to my goals.

All I want to point your attention to is clarity. I labeled myself as an artist and creative, and automatically assumed that I needed to live a typical lifestyle associated with creative professions.

Many people make the same mistake but in their own unique way. For example, a friend of mine is a business coach, and she's doing very well with her brand now. She's doing so well because she is simply being herself and embracing her authenticity. At the beginning of her journey, she tried hard to be like other business coaches in her space. She wanted to seem very professional and have the same branding as most people in her field. Yet, she could never attract the type of people she really wanted to work with (spiritual teachers and holistic practitioners). I had a look at her content and asked her, "Why are you trying so hard to be exactly the same as all those business consultants who are in the B2B (business to business) space if it's not really aligned with what you want and who you want to attract?"

So, she re-branded her business based on her true desires. She unleashed the courage to be herself and began attracting the client base she wanted to help and work with. Not that what she was doing before was wrong, but it just wasn't for her. Simultaneously, if someone wants to attract a business type of client or do very high-ticket deals, and it's what they seek, then, of course, the way they build their brand should be different. It's all about alignment.

We often think that just copying what other people did and had success with will solve our problems. But in reality, we need to find that inner courage to dive deep.

In the following chapters, we will be exploring more techniques to help you get clear on your life mission and philosophy (applicable to all kinds of goals, dreams, and desires), so don't worry for now. Just keep asking yourself, "Is it really for me? Will this serve me in the long run?"

Sometimes we have good intentions, and we think we are on the right path, but something inside us feels off. That feeling often indicates the lack of alignment or an inner battle. Your logical mind thinks and assumes this is right for you, but your heart and soul rebel. Tune in and listen to those feelings. They want to guide you towards shaping your new self-image: the self-image that will lead you towards long-lasting transformation, freedom, and success.

For example, my friend had good intentions. She purchased a program on how to become a successful consultant, and the program was created by someone who did very well for himself, and so did most of his students.

She followed each lesson and was pleased to see that the business training also talked a lot about mindset, the LOA, and even self-image. However, back then, she didn't know how to create her unique self-image and unconsciously copied what everyone in the program was doing. Then she began manifesting, but it didn't feel in alignment with what she truly wanted. So, she had to go back and make some re-adjustments. She feels very grateful for the lessons learned and uses it as her brand story to help people in their businesses by being authentic.

In my case, my old "party all night" lifestyle didn't help me improve my performance or my writing routine.

The Science of Becoming a Truly New Person

When I was in my nightlife mode, I wasn't very productive during the day, and I didn't feel like eating healthy food or exercising. That old version of me had to go. However, right now, looking back, I'm grateful I experienced it because it made me who I am today. I realized what I value in life and what makes me happy. And since I had already experienced the partying and nightlife, I felt like I could close that chapter and lead a more organized life.

Once again, this isn't about changing who you are. I'm still that curious and creative person, but with a different self-image. It's all about becoming a different version of yourself while unleashing your full potential. A version that fully aligns with your mission. Your reality is just a delayed reflection of your new self-image and how you think and feel.

Now, people always ask me, "But what if I don't know what I want? What if I just want freedom. What am I supposed to do?"

Be OK with "not knowing what to do." Stop desperately searching for answers. If you know that freedom is essential to you, focus on exploring what it really means to you and how you can experience more of it every day. Align your thoughts, feelings, and actions with it. Write down all the activities that make you feel free and intend to do more of them. As you do them, be grateful and amplify the feelings of freedom. As you begin to focus on what makes you feel free, you will attract more space and different ideas to experience it. Create a self-image of a person who lives a free lifestyle and see what happens. However, if you focus too much on "not knowing" and "searching," you might never experience that what is important to you - freedom.

Another question I often get asked is, "How can I change my environment if I can't afford to move to another city or apartment?"

My answer is that the most important thing is always inner change. For example, one of my readers was sharing his apartment with other people, and back then, he couldn't afford to live by himself. But instead of focusing on the fact that his roommates weren't his ideal role model avatars (to put it mildly), he decided to focus on what he could control. He began making some changes in his room and decorated it the way it made him feel good. He chose to be grateful for the fact that he had a bed and a place to live. Instead of sitting on the couch and complaining like his old roomies used to do, he chose to go to the gym. Very soon, he began attracting new opportunities, including a better job and a new apartment. This is the power of changing your inner world and doing the best you can with what's available to you. And the good news is that your mindset is relatively easy to control.

Another reader said to me, "The problem I have with trying to change myself is that I start out the right way, with the right intentions about changing. But then I end up with the shiny object syndrome. For example, I keep wanting to get a better job, change the city again, or even change the way I look again. It can get very frustrating."

So, this is a pattern I very often see - we force ourselves to keep changing, and we try hard to change. We already discussed it in the beginning so, I'm pretty sure my answer won't come as a surprise to my readers.

"First of all, you think you have a problem (however, you may see your reality as if you were just testing different options in life to see what you like). And so, you keep looking for a solution. You think you have to change yourself or keep doing more to change faster or to change again.

My tip would be to try to focus on the positive as much as you can and release the need to change yourself. Instead, *focus on becoming*. The good news is that we are always becoming something, and it all starts with the quality of our thoughts, actions, and feelings.

Accept yourself just the way you are and focus on finding peace and harmony within. Then, ask yourself if you really feel like going after a new job or moving houses. Do it if it feels right or if you feel curious or excited about it. In other words, do it if you're driven by a positive emotion. If, however, you feel like you're stuck in constantly escaping from something, it might be worth finding out what that is so that you can transform it into something positive. Even changing your self-talk to something more encouraging or empowering may be a great start for the consistent practice that will shift your identity."

Chapter 2 - Release Your Old Programs and Stop Fighting Yourself (The Art of Manifesting from a Place of Neutrality)

Focus creates attraction. And we all manifest some outcomes. The question is, why do we tend to focus on the negative instead of the positive?

For example, a bestselling author may launch yet another fantastic book awaited by many fans. The book has many 5-star reviews and then, someone posts a nasty 1-star without even providing any constructive feedback, just bashing the book. The writer may end up with some negative thoughts such as, "Maybe this book really isn't that good. Maybe I need to make some changes to it"

In reality, it's just people posting what they think, and some of them may have a bad day or simply didn't enjoy the way the book was written. Different strokes for different folks. Yet, it is so human to keep focusing on and reminding ourselves of the negative.

It's a negative hypnotic trance when we focus on what is not serving us. The good news is that this process can be reversed, and we can focus on the positive if we choose to. It all comes down to understanding the self-reprogramming cycle and using it to your advantage.

The self-reprogramming cycle starts with a simple thought. For example, "Someone didn't like my book (or something else)."

You can choose to accept it or not. If you don't accept it, it just becomes a simple, "OK, we have freedom of speech, thank God for that, and people are allowed to share their thoughts, experiences, and opinions. Besides, even the best of the best books get negative reviews. OK, let's move on." Of course, the thought can also be accepted, invited, and expanded on. "Oh no. I think they are right. Maybe this book sucks, and so I suck, and once again, I'm wasting my time on doing something that wasn't meant for me. Why can't I just...?" and boom, we are in a negative hypnotic trance.

You attach a negative meaning and emotion to your thoughts. You begin to like and entertain the thought, and you accept it, even though it puts you in a negative and doubtful state of being. Or you know you don't like it, and you start to resist it, and what you resist persists. So, the end result is still the same. You end up thinking you did something wrong, are not worthy of success, or whatever negative memories and experiences got triggered.

This may seem innocent at first and, in reality, could be harmless if nipped in the bud (which is possible with a well-developed self-awareness). Over time, your predominant thought, such as "I'm not good enough, they are coming after me," becomes a belief. And then your Reticular Activating System (RAS) gets programmed for it, and then it starts looking for proof (consciously or unconsciously). Your mind begins to reject anything else and just focuses on the negative.

For example, "Elena sucks. She will never make it as a writer. Oh, and she sucks at everything really, so no matter what she does, it will suck too, and everyone will laugh."

As soon as it becomes a deeply ingrained belief, Elena's RAS leads her to look for proof, and she will find more negative reviews to confirm it.

When it comes to seeking out negativity, we are all naturally talented at this - even us positive, self-development and spirituality people!

Come on; there must be more bad reviews. Let's find them all and feel worse! You see, I told you, you sucked. Who do you think you are?

Then, what was just a thought, and then a belief, becomes a firm conviction that can even manifest negativity and resistance in other projects that Elena decides to do.

While the example above may seem a little bit exaggerated, this is more or less what happens in our minds. I'm sure you can relate to it, no matter what your goals are, or what kind of work you do, or passion/hobby you pursue.

The good news is we can consciously change our cycle simply by understanding how it works and reverse-engineering it in a positive way that programs us and our self-image to focus on and automatically attract positivity into our lives.

Once again, let's have a look at this cycle:

Thought – Opinion – Belief – Conviction

(Please note that a conviction is a firm belief that may take more inner work to eliminate. But there's still hope,

Release Your Old Programs and Stop Fighting Yourself

and many people have managed to release their negative convictions.)

Let's say I want to program myself with "Elena is a good author, and she should keep writing."

I can now consciously positively repeat the whole cycle. I start off with a thought; I add positive feelings and emotions to it. I visualize myself writing or talking to my readers and feeling good about what I do.

I intend to work with the whole cycle, and my RAS gets naturally programmed to look for ways to confirm that Elena is indeed a prolific writer. One of the ways to do so is to focus on things I want to see.

This is a compelling self-reprogramming cycle. Your new self-image needs to focus (very carefully) on what you choose to accept in your reality. You don't panic. You don't turn other people's opinions into your personal conviction.

Knowing how this cycle works can genuinely help you focus on the positive by becoming positive and embracing all things positive, using your mind, body, heart, and soul.

Release Your Old Programs and Stop Fighting Yourself

Now that you know how this cycle works, I highly recommend you start practicing it as much as you can. I always say that our triggers can be our healers. So, whenever you discover that something bothers you (perhaps something happened and triggered a negative memory), write it down in your journal. Of course, we don't want to focus on it or dwell on it. All we want to do is to figure out our negative cycle and turn it into something positive. Once again, we are naturally talented at using the negative process of programming. It's just what we are good at, and it doesn't take much effort to think negatively.

So, if you are new to this work, it may make you feel mentally, emotionally, and spiritually tired at first. But it is like training a muscle. With a bit of practice and following the guidance from this chapter, you too can embrace your positive self-image. You can start to become what you desire to attract into your life. Now, you can also feel grateful for any negative emotions and thoughts that arise. Not because you want more of them, but because you understand the power of this phrase: *our biggest triggers are our most prominent healers*!

Chapter 3 -When Being Driven or Motivated May Turn Against You (The Hidden Dangers of Self-Improvement)

Why are you on this journey? Why are you doing this? What are your goals and desires? Why and how did you come up with them?

Are you taking action from a place of scarcity, lack, or trying to prove something to others? Do you seek validation or approval?

Or do you choose to manifest and take action from a relaxed alignment, natural confidence, and authenticity?

In other words, is your intention pure?

In this chapter, you will gain a deeper understanding of what acting from fear does to you and why the new version of yourself needs to learn how to let go.

The truth is that most (if not all) actions you take from fear will always result in more fear. I consider myself lucky because I discovered this concept in the early stages of my writing journey. You see, I came across someone I really admired.

This author did exceptionally well for himself, and he'd written dozens of bestselling books in the self-help space, as well as several fiction novels. I quickly realized he was probably one of the most successful in the space, so I began to study him and even asked him if he could mentor me. He didn't reply for several months, so I assumed he was probably getting a ton of emails from "wannabes" like myself back then, and I just moved on. I still felt happy I at least attempted to reach out and seek mentorship. As they say, if you don't ask, the answer is always no!

So, I felt happy when he replied to me after nearly a year. He said he was on a healing journey and had taken some time off. He also said he wasn't offering any mentoring or consulting but that the only piece of advice he could give me (so that I could be a happy and prolific writer) was:

- Never take action from a place of lack, and never write just to show off or prove yourself in front of others. Don't use your books to seek fame, approval, or recognition. And never get attached to positive reviews and bestseller badges. You don't want to end up in a never-ending chasing.

He then briefly told me his story. Even though his fears and insecurities gave him a great start and foundation for

When Being Driven or Motivated May Turn Against You

his writing career and his own publishing brand, he still felt empty once he built his way to the top. He lost his purpose completely. This is why he decided to take almost a year off and do some inner healing. He also felt it was the right thing to do, especially if he wanted to continue writing books related to self-development.

Back then, I was still something between a wannabe and a newbie, and what this author told me really made me check my intentions and what was driving me at that time. As you can probably imagine from my previous stories, I had different careers and passion projects before my writing, and most (if not all of them) were driven by my fears and insecurities. I nearly took my negative emotions to my new creative endeavors – my writing.

To this day, I am forever grateful for the advice I received from that author. I definitely consider him my mentor, just because of this one little email reply he decided to send me.

How does it all translate to aligning your self-image with what you desire to attract into your life? It's simple.

Some people think there is no significant difference between action and intention. However, intention comes first. Your actions (intentions that manifest, or intentions that can be seen because of what you decide to do) come from intentions (source of your actions).

For example, a person may have this negative belief driving their intention: "I don't have clients, money, fame, or recognition."

So, they take massive action from a place of, "I need to be successful no matter what. I will show them what I'm worth. I'll be successful, and they will come. They will see me and give me the praise I deserve."

I have seen this pattern over and over again. And I'm saying this from a place of love because I understand how it feels, and you already know I have been there many times before I could finally learn my lesson. For example, in my old business, I wanted to make money so that those who didn't believe in me (like old friends and even some family members) would finally approve of me and praise me.

"Look at me, look at me! Look, look. See, see? I told you! You didn't believe in me and now – look! I'm someone. I'm so successful, and you? What have you done with your life?"

When Being Driven or Motivated May Turn Against You

And while this misaligned fear-based and insecurity-driven motivation gave me some financial success back then, it wasn't lasting, and it also resulted in a massive burnout.

I even unconsciously used this pattern at the beginning of my online journey. I felt needy and insecure, and readers could sense that. I remember that when I first created my website, I shared a story of how a school teacher laughed at me and how I now use it as a motivation to be successful, to *show them* what I'm really capable of.

Luckily, the Universe guided me and sent me the mentor who helped me understand the most aligned way to focus on my writing.

But I also noticed that whenever I took action from a relaxed, abundant place (with a loved-based intention), I would actually take action that resulted in success (and fulfillment). I often had to work less, or somehow, I would find myself being more productive without even trying to do more.

It goes back to what I mentioned in the intro. You are already good enough, and there is no need to change or improve yourself. However, you can choose to and focus on becoming and transforming, which is a journey in itself, and it's a journey you cannot judge with your logical and very often fear-based mind.

Most people focus on actions, not on intentions. Or they take actions without understanding their intentions. For example, in sales, some people try to master the latest persuasion technique to get that quick sale.

(I remember working in sales and desperately trying to master the latest "influence trick" and whatnot, or following up with potential clients way too fast, and therefore coming across as being very needy).

Of course, I'm not putting down the desire to learn new things, especially if it's required in the line of work you do. However, whatever it is that you do, what is your intention behind it?

For example, someone who intends to make more sales could come from a love-based intention to help more people with the specific products/services they sell. In alignment, they could spend more time trying to understand the people they sell to and what *they* really desire, and what motivates *them*. While talking to their prospects, a salesperson can choose to determine whether and how they can help them and then select

When Being Driven or Motivated May Turn Against You

products and services that align with that. Fear-based intentions often align with: *What can I get?* Whereas love-based intentions align with: *What can I give?*

Unfortunately, fear-based intentions drive so many of us in so many different areas of our lives!

What about health and fitness? So many people take action from a place of fear, "What if I put on weight or lose muscle?" This is why so many people look for fad diets and why magic weight loss pills and fear-based solutions are always so tempting.

In our LOA space, people often jump into new techniques because they are driven by the fear of manifesting the negative, or perhaps not manifesting fast enough or comparing themselves to other manifestors.

And in self-development, people desperately try to improve themselves. But the actions that follow, more often than not, are taken from a place of fear and "I'm not good enough." By now, I'm sure you understand the pattern.

And this is a very short-term strategy. Whenever you feel fear, and it drives you to take action, it actually re-wires your brain for more fear.

When Being Driven or Motivated May Turn Against You

You take action to try and supplement some kind of lack. Simultaneously, acting immediately when in a state of fear means that you are escaping that fear (and action can also be a distraction).

For example, smoking a cigarette, eating unhealthy foods, or drinking alcohol are ways to escape fear or anxiety.

The mechanism is the same as, for example, a business owner desperately setting up online ads, straight from a place of fear to try to get more and make more money in their business. And very often, all that happens is that their ad spend goes up. Still, they can't make any more profit unless they somehow come across some marketing magician or a super unique strategy. But, even with those things, the fear-based actions will never lead to long-lasting success.

What happens when you repress the most significant problem (fear and scarcity) is that, sooner or later, it will come back in another pair of shoes. Taking action from a place of scarcity (while the primary intention is fear) always puts people off. Whether it's talking to a prospective client on the phone, sending an email, creating an advertisement to attract business, or doing a job interview.

When Being Driven or Motivated May Turn Against You

Your reality knows what is inside you, and the energy never lies. The secret is in mindful scanning of what is going inside you. Whenever you feel anxiety or fear, feel it and accept it, but don't take immediate action from such energy.

The first thing to do is to surrender to it so that you can dissipate what's no longer serving you. You can mindfully express how you feel so that you don't suppress it.

Constant suppression doesn't solve anything. It only multiplies it and makes it come back in another moment so that eventually, it becomes a negative subconscious pattern.

Question your fear, pain, and negative feelings so that you can consciously separate yourself from them and realize that *you are not your fear.*

The following questions can help:

- Can I allow this to be? (Now, you will feel more of it so that you can fully feel it for the last time and let it go.)

- Can I let it go? Can I finally let it go? When can I let it go? Now? In five minutes, five weeks, five years?

You may not feel so good the first time you do it, and I know, I know, many LOA people, like us, can feel resistance. Aren't we supposed to do things that make us feel good?

The answer is yes. However, understanding our fears and negative intentions will help us embrace our positive self-image in a way that is pretty much automatic. In other words, we need to eliminate the negative roots of our problems that make us manifest what we don't want.

Becoming reactive to our fears can never help us long-term because it re-wires us to take action when there is fear. Because of that, we find it hard to be driven to take action when things are well.

Now, the old Elena who just wanted to achieve, achieve, and achieve (to show other people what she was capable of) would just laugh at the above paragraphs. She would say, "But so many successful people say they were driven by fear, and look what they have achieved!"

Yes, this is true, and fear can drive us at the beginning of our journey and make us high achievers in society's eye. The real question is, what will be the price for success? Happiness, health, peace of mind?

I don't know about you, but my intention is to keep fulfilling my mission and peacefully achieving it while creating balance and abundance in all areas of my life.

When Being Driven or Motivated May Turn Against You

My old self-image always had fear-based intentions that led to fear-based actions. This is how I learned my lesson, and this is why I'm writing this book. I know that taking action from a place of fear and lack eventually always leads to more pain and anxiety. Even if you manifest what you wanted, for example, you get a new home or a new car, or a new job, you may still feel you're not good enough, and so you get stuck in this energy. Your old fears may disappear for a while only to come back later in another situation that triggers you.

Of course, as I said in the introduction, I don't want to indoctrinate my readers into any specific way of thinking if it's not suitable for them, so take what you like and reject the rest.

If you feel like it's too much to take in for now, simply intend to become more mindful and aware and keep asking yourself what drives you? Love or fear? Is your intention to keep getting, or is it to keep giving while creating more positive energy around you?

I write for different reader avatars. Some readers come from spirituality, and they really resonate with love and fear-based concepts. Some readers are coming from self-improvement, success, or business, and the self-image ideas they were taught may be a little bit different than the concepts described in this chapter. Many successful entrepreneurs, authors, professionals, and high performers got started on their success journey because of fear (or being sick and tired of being sick and tired). And it got them to a particular stage of success. In this case, fear can be a good thing, but only initially.

However, lasting success magnified by happiness and fulfillment arrives when a person replaces fear-based intentions with love-based intentions that lead to love-based actions. So, design your new self-image from a place of love. (You can thank me later.)

I highly recommend you protect your mind and your energy from negative influences. In one of my earlier books, I came up with a phrase: *stop scrolling and start manifesting* (I'm considering writing a short eBook just on this topic and how social media can reverberate on our manifestations).

Ask yourself how much time you spend on social media (or in front of a TV) while being in a mindless state and easily influenced by negativity?

I'm ashamed to admit how many products I bought out of fear because I saw a fear-based advertisement somewhere online or on TV (somehow, those late-night

When Being Driven or Motivated May Turn Against You

infomercials would always get me!). Many marketers behind those ads and products understand the power of fear and that fear-based marketing gets people to buy more and faster. Not all marketing is terrible; many loved-based marketers create ads differently, and again, it all boils down to the power of intention.

But now, looking back at my purchases, the best investments I made in myself were the ones I got from a place of love while feeling curious and excited about what I was going to discover.

Instead of mindlessly buying out of fear, thinking, "maybe one day I can use this product," or "I'm not good enough unless I buy it."

To discover your intention, ask yourself, from what place do I invest my time and money? Is it love or fear? Design your new self-image in alignment with positive, love-based, and empowering intentions, and watch your reality reflect your inner transformations by sending you more beautiful people, events, and circumstances.

Chapter 4 - How to Create Your New Joyful Habits & Aligned Discipline (and the One Crucial Thing Most People Miss)

I used to be against habits because I thought I would be mindless or unconscious: just doing the same things all over again. I'm a creative and spiritual person who truly values a sense of freedom and expression, and I used to find it very hard to follow schedules.

And, as such, I really used to resist all kinds of habits. Yes, I heard of people who take cold showers at 5 am every morning, and I heard of people who run every day, even if it's raining or snowing. And I heard of people who wake up and make a green smoothie and do yoga. While I admired all those stories and found them inspiring, I always thought, "Yeah, they can do it because they are disciplined and organized. I'm more of a person who loves freedom, so habits are not for me."

Little did I realize that:

How to Create Your New Joyful Habits & Aligned Discipline

- My own resistance to change was blocking my new self-image (after all, I desired to be a productive, ambitious, and prolific writer who writes every day).

- I thought of habits in terms of black and white. For example, I either wake up at 4 am and have a run, a green smoothie, and a cold shower, or I sleep till noon and don't do anything.

- I was being way too focused on what instead of who.

For example, what other people choose to do as their habits and what works for them may not necessarily be for me. So, I kept asking myself:

- Who do I need to become?

- How would the new version of myself react to the word "habit?"

- Does it have to be all black or white? Can't I just find something I could align with my lifestyle and values (freedom, flexibility, and creativity)?

Yes, it can be very inspiring to see other people do their habits and challenges and succeed with their schedules. But it can also make us postpone our own mindful habit creation that will align us with who we need to become.

How to Create Your New Joyful Habits & Aligned Discipline

Once again, I had to remind myself of the basics:

- It's all about becoming the best version of yourself (while already feeling good enough!) and experimenting with it.

- It's not the action but the energy you bring. It's always the intention behind the action that's important.

I said to myself, "OK, Elena. You already have certain beliefs about what you need to do to be successful or manifest your desires. You have created some conditions for yourself. You now eat healthier, and you don't party. Yet you don't give yourself the permission to just be, and experience your new self fully. Something is blocking you. What can you do to create simple habits to help you:

- Improve your energy on all levels?

- Get better focus and clarity?

- Wake up excited?

- Feel like a winner after doing it?"

Now, I'll be the first one to admit that I'm not into cold showers (even though I know they have many health benefits and may align with many people's goals), nor super early am clubs.

How to Create Your New Joyful Habits & Aligned Discipline

So, I decided to focus on simple daily habits that I enjoy, including:

1. Daily Emotional Freedom Technique (EFT) tapping. I look forward to doing it every evening, and it helps me relax and sleep better. At the same time, I use it to release stuck energy and emotions that hold me back from reaching the next level on my journey. I always end up recommending EFT to my readers! A great book to help you get started is the *Tapping Solution* by Nick Ortner, or you can simply look up some videos on YouTube to learn the basics. Learning EFT to work on yourself doesn't require too much time to master.

I don't need to force myself to do it. I look forward to doing it. After I'm done releasing what I no longer need, I feel so much better (physically, emotionally, spiritually, and mentally). EFT always helps me get to the next level of my journey.

2. Getting up early on weekdays. So, as you know from my earlier stories, I decided to stop partying and living an excessive social life as it wasn't my path anyway (I'm an introvert, really, so it wasn't

that hard). But I still had some old, misaligned habits of waking up way too late. I knew I had to change them. So, I set up a new waking up time at around 7 am. Not too late, and not too early. Just perfect for my journey and goals. I could finally get the most important writing done before noon and could then go for a walk, have lunch and have the afternoons to focus on other projects as well.

3. Daily walks in nature (including some runs without forcing myself to do them, more like a bonus!).

Thanks to adding this little habit (and combining it with EFT in the evenings), I could finally heal my insomnia. I could just go to bed, fall asleep and wake up feeling refreshed the following day.

Small habits always lead to significant transformations, and it's not about blindly following the practices that other people have for themselves.

Also, true freedom is created on the foundation of the mindful discipline. Even creative people like me can find the balance between freedom and discipline. In fact, it

How to Create Your New Joyful Habits & Aligned Discipline

doesn't even feel like "having to be more disciplined" anymore. All three of the habits I created for myself (up early to write, daily walks/exercise, and EFT) align with one another and help me stay in peace and alignment to stay focused on my new endeavors and enjoy every step of the journey.

Your habits also determine your self-image. Ask yourself, do you treat yourself the way you deserve? Yes, habits and mindful discipline are a form of self-care. It doesn't have to be about self-torture or forcing yourself into doing something just because it's popular on social media or everyone in the self-development community is doing it.

Your beliefs determine your habits and how you choose to treat yourself. Your thoughts also give you possible excuses and resistance as to why you can't create your new, empowering habits. I genuinely hope that my story can inspire you to create your own daily habits that are aligned with what you desire to attract and how you desire to feel.

You can choose to be in unity with your beliefs by creating empowering habits around them. Give yourself some time to play around and experiment. You may get

How to Create Your New Joyful Habits & Aligned Discipline

inspired by some of my patterns (yes, I'm a big fan of EFT, and from my experience, I can tell you that it's one of the most time-effective practices you can integrate into your daily life!), or choose your own. Remember, though, proper alignment comes when you use your actions to affirm what you desire. This results in you manifesting excellent outcomes and transformations.

And if you still feel the resistance, remember this - getting started may be a little bit hard. But you can choose to do something that makes you feel like a winner after you have done it. It's OK to stretch your comfort zone and expand your mindset a little bit!

Small habits around your self-care, new skill-set, or passion can be easy to implement and make you feel like a winner if they align with your goals and vision. Self-care means that you are important to yourself and that you are becoming a better version of yourself all the time.

A few simple, daily habits helped me eliminate insomnia and anxiety while making me feel good. Positive emotions are essential to manifest our desires.

In contrast, before creating my new, empowering habits, I was:

How to Create Your New Joyful Habits & Aligned Discipline

- Overthinking everything ("What's the point of making this habit and wasting the energy I could use to write?" – but in the end, I could never get anything done because my overthinking mind was draining my energy!)

- Suffered from insomnia ("Oh my god, it's probably some karma from past lives times coming back at me, or maybe someone is sending me negative energies - they are coming after me!").

- Oversleeping (because I felt a bit anxious or sleepy, and I could never fall asleep until 3 or 4 am).

But now, thanks to my new daily habits, I feel better about myself and everything around me. I'm more productive (without pushing and trying to do more), and I have more freedom (one of my highest values in life).

Now, I have more time to keep learning more about my new passion – EFT. I am even considering doing a certified course because, due to my new habits and schedule, finding the time and saving the money to do it doesn't seem like such a faraway goal as it did a couple of years ago.

Also, create powerful habits for the mind. Whenever some negative thoughts arise (or any thought you feel is coming from your old self), thank it for trying to protect you and intend to let it go. With this approach, eventually, it will dissolve. Ask yourself - does your new self wants to keep suffering? Wouldn't it be better to do something to free your mind from the negative and align it to the positive?

Also, do your old attachments and expectations make you suffer? Whatever you experience inside you, your external reality will (sooner or later) reflect. Suffering happens because you identify with something that is constantly changing, e.g., fame, success, business revenue, praise from your boss.

Pain happens in your body, but suffering is when you feel permanent pain in your mind. You start identifying with whatever happens to you, and all your awareness is tied up to your thoughts.

For example, a person may identify with: "This is my job, this is my business, this is my success, this is my income level. When it goes down or goes away, I suffer because it's like a part of me was taken away! I worked so hard for it!"

Luckily, when you start to observe something, you no longer identify with it. Instead of living it and performing it, you are in the audience watching it (and observing the person who thinks it). Go beyond it. For example, right now, I caught myself with some "old thoughts" such as, "I think I'm making it too complicated, what if they (my readers) won't understand me?" and then, "Oh, what if they think it's too simplistic and they say they heard it all before?"

But now, those thoughts don't get me off track. I still keep writing; I tell myself, "OK, thank you, old Elena, for trying to protect me! But I'm a new person now. Hey, it's just some old thought. It's actually pretty funny because if I choose to entertain it, I might as well hide under my bed!"

Sometimes, I use my imagination to turn such a thought into something funny. I make a serious voice saying to myself, "Oh my God Elena, what have you done? They are coming, they are coming, they will find you, they will come to your house, and they will tell you you suck. You'd better hide under your bed now!"

Laughter and turning negative thoughts into jokes (if you find it suitable, of course) may do the trick. It always works well for me, and it helps me release the emotional charge of many of my old thoughts so that I no longer identify with them.

Take an inventory of your thoughts, audit them and watch them. Who's thinking those thoughts? Your new self? Or your old self? Thank your old self for trying to protect you and give it a well-deserved retirement on the beach. It already worked hard for you at some stage. But now, you choose to think, feel and act in alignment with your new reality!

Chapter 5 - Why Your New-Self Image Wants to Test You (and When Negative Outcomes Are Not Really That Negative)

Have you ever experienced obstacles on your journey? You started off excited, you had good intentions and were visualizing the positive, yet obstacles appeared. You felt like everything was against you. Or maybe you did something wrong, or feel that something is wrong with you, your karma, or energy.

First things first - I don't think there's anything wrong with you.

Oh, and some energy work is always a good idea if you have a good healer (but this is not the point of this chapter).

My point is - if you blame yourself and your energy for every obstacle, it's kind of a negative pattern as well, and let me tell you this - you didn't do anything wrong. You just need to understand the Universal patterns and why and how they may attempt to test you. Stop all those self-guilt and self-blame trips right here and right now! (Unless, for whatever reason, feeling guilty aligns with your new self-image and the desired results for your future manifestations.)

Every time you have an intention to manifest something, the Universe, life, and your new self, want to test you. Focus on what you can control - your attitude! Yes, I know; it's hard to be grateful if things don't go your way.

But... how can you know the right way?

A way is just a way. Be sure to stay positively focused on your destination.

Life will arrange everything and take the path to least resistance. If it gives you tests, it wants to check your attitude and reaction. It wants you to confirm your goals and desires. It wants to check if you are committed to carrying on, despite the obstacles. It doesn't want you to give up, but it may want you to give in and surrender, accepting that things don't always have to go your way to get you where you desire to be. Also, challenges and obstacles will make your new self-image stronger so that you are fully equipped to manage your new reality as soon as it manifests.

The Universe is an extensive, kind intelligence with its own unique ways, and our minds are small, logical minds. The Universe always knows the better way, and sometimes our small minds can't understand what is going on. The most important thing is to trust the process.

First, you make an intention. For example, you want to double your income.

The so-called coordination or testing period comes because the Universe wants to test you and check if your internal world is really harmonious with the intention you stated. Only then comes the fruition stage, and you can enjoy your new reality. The problem is that our limited, logical minds want to skip the test period. We set intentions and try hard to think of the best way to get there or the next milestone on our journeys, and when things go south, we feel discouraged!

So, remember the formula:

Intention – Test – Fruition

To speed up your manifestation process, you can speed up your new, authentic self-image creation by owning your perception.

Your own attitude and the meaning you attach to things that happen after you set out your intention will determine how your journey unfolds.

Why Your New Self-Image Want to Test You

For example, a self-employed coach is typically attracting five new clients a month. His new goal is to attract ten new clients a month. So, he sets an intention. After setting his new intention, suddenly, it seems like his business goes down, and he only got one client this month. He immediately starts thinking, "OMG, something must be wrong with me, and it's not working out for me! Why docs it always work for other people but not for me?"

He decides to accept the situation yet uses all his creative energy to focus on what he desires. He doesn't resist what's happening – he just takes it as a test that is needed on his journey. The Universe knows what kinds of circumstances you need to go through to become the stronger version of yourself that fully aligns with your desires.

So, instead of panicking that his business is going down when it was supposed to improve, he chooses to think:

- Ah, OK, it makes sense. This month, I will have less work so that I can prepare myself fully to be able to work with more clients soon!

Why Your New Self-Image Want to Test You

- Now, I have more time to finish that course I wanted to do because I know I will have more awesome tools and techniques to help my new clients.

- Oh, and when I get to the stage of having more clients every month, I will need an assistant. Now, this month, I have less coaching work to do, so I can finally hire and train someone. Yes, maybe I will need to reduce my expenses this month, but I know it will be worth it in the long run. Thank you, Universe, for this test. If you say I need a little bit of a break from coaching work this month to focus on the bigger picture, let's do this.

Three months pass, and the coach easily attracts 15-20 new clients a month, and they are all ready to enroll in his most expensive programs!

This is a real story, by the way!

New energy and acceptance behind what may seem like an obstacle can create opportunities in alignment with our original intentions.

Become aware of your own complaining. Catch yourself and don't judge it. Simply ask yourself: Is it really worth complaining? Or can I use my inner energy more productively? Will complaining even change anything?

Why Your New Self-Image Want to Test You

Would my new self complain? Trust the Universe, trust your unique self and trust your new process.

Chapter 6 - When Abundance Doesn't Follow Confidence

True, authentic abundance follows true confidence. The keyword here is authentic. At the same time, true, lasting abundance doesn't follow confidence that is shallow and false.

You see, in the past, I thought I needed to have a massive following on Instagram or other platforms; otherwise, nobody would get my books or pay any attention to what I was doing. For a long time, I thought of myself as someone invisible and someone unworthy of any meaningful engagement. That limiting story became my limiting belief, then my limiting conviction that eventually drove all my motivations. I wanted to "change myself" and become someone I wasn't. Just to try to be heard.

Back then, I used to buy courses from different online gurus because, in a way, I was desperate to figure out how to become one myself. And it would never work. I even attempted product launches (lots of money, time, and effort went into all this) with no results. Something felt off all the time.

At that time, I was trying to be persuasive, and I was trying to pretend. I was trying to be someone I wasn't.

I wanted to be 'hypey' because someone told me that was the way to go.

As a result, I burned out. And so I went on a journey to really figure out what was going on. Finally, I came across various experts who seemed very authentic and whose energy really resonated with me. I quickly noticed they had genuine confidence. They didn't have any fancy websites or branding. They were just being themselves and were doing the best they could with what they had. Those people really inspired me to be myself and do things that felt authentic to me while attracting people with similar energy.

Because of that, I no longer had to use all my creative energy to pretend to be someone I wasn't or to pose online. That gave me a lot of inner freedom. It also gave me the tools to ease up on myself, stop trying to be perfect, and dissolve all those self-guilt trips of what I felt I should be doing because everyone around me was doing it.

Of course, if you really feel inspired by someone and it feels authentic to you, go for it!

When Abundance Doesn't Follow Confidence

When you are yourself and act from your authentic, confident energy, it automatically helps you ease up on self-blame and manifest faster. Simply do the best you can right now, using the tools you have available to you.

Self-blame is not helping you and is not spiritual. The Universe/God/Source wants us to use our mistakes as lessons. I remember feeling so mad at myself (while blaming myself and feeling guilty) because I "wasted" time and money on projects that didn't work out and weren't even for me in the first place.

I had thoughts like, "I should have just focused on my writing instead." Then I would feel guilty about feeling guilty. Finally, I had to learn to love my old self because my old self got me to where I am today, my new self!

We can rebel against our self-blame or calmly say, "Ok, so what's the lesson here to learn?"

There is no rush. Every day is for you to practice your authentic confidence. You can also use the following meditation.

How to Connect with Your Authentic Confidence and Your New, Empowered Self-Image

This meditation will help you connect your heart and mind together.

We use our minds so much more than our hearts. Even when it comes to creating our self-image, we tend to over-think the next level and what we should be like from the outside, but we underestimate our hearts.

The heart can connect to the quantum field and help you find answers that your logical mind wouldn't have any access to. Sometimes logic doesn't make sense for our long-term wellbeing because we make decisions from a minimal space of limited consciousness.

This meditation becomes more potent if you do it for 30 days straight (mornings and evenings are the best time). Let's do this!

- First of all, you want to relax and feel a pleasant warmth and tingling sensation in your heart. Think of something or someone that makes you feel good.

- See and feel happy, abundant, and joyous as the warm light expands from your heart into all parts of your body. Feel the warmth. Your heart is already sending you

When Abundance Doesn't Follow Confidence

signals and the information that your body and mind will process and reveal to you when the time is right.

- Sit up straight with your spine erect, take a deep breath and close your eyes. Inhale into your stomach. Exhale and relax. Take one more breath in, exhale and let it all out. Take one final breath in. As you exhale, feel every single fiber of your being relax.

- Put your right hand over your heart and take another deep breath. Exhale and relax. Feel your palm connecting to your heart. Can you feel the warmth of your heart? Feel your heart getting warmer and warmer.

- Once again, feel another wave of warm light expanding all over your body. Repeat the process and imagine the light around your heart getting lighter and lighter while embracing the feelings of peace, harmony, calmness, and warmth. You don't have to try to think about your solutions and answers. You already have everything you need. It's all inside you. It has always been inside you!

- Feel the nice heat spreading all over your body and expanding and feel it pulsating around your heart.

- Take another deep breath in. Feel the power originating from your heart, expanding beyond your body. Feel the ball of nice, warm energy expanding from your heart. Do this one more time, inhale and exhale. This ball is now expanding. You may even hear it make some noises.

- Think of your new self. Your new self-image. Feel this ball of energy expanding and touching your new self. Feel connected to your new self. See the different versions of you, including your old selves that got you where you are today. Imagine this ball touching them as well. See them smiling and happy. Exhale and send them love. Now, look at yourself, learn to see yourself and take a step back from yourself and see yourself happy. See yourself succeeding, see yourself enjoying life every day, see yourself joyous, happy, loving. Give yourself some love. Now, tell yourself you love yourself. Tell yourself you trust yourself. Take a deep breath, and as you exhale, send this massive ball of love to yourself.

- Now, slowly, open your eyes. Remain in a relaxed state for a few minutes and then gradually proceed to your daily activities.

You can use this meditation whenever you feel like your logical mind needs a well-deserved vacation, and your heart deserves a promotion at your company!

It's all about getting in touch with your heart. Once the connection is re-activated or amplified, you will see new

When Abundance Doesn't Follow Confidence

opportunities coming to you; problems suddenly start solving themselves, you are more receptive, money starts to flow your way, you no longer worry about the things you used to worry about. You just begin to trust yourself and the Universe. This is true, authentic confidence that will help you go out and do what you want almost effortlessly.

You will save a lot of energy that is wasted on pretending, trying, and pushing, and you will be able to use it to be more creative and productive in alignment with what you wish to manifest.

Also, it's time to say no to not feeling good enough, judging yourself, and demanding more of yourself.

We got conditioned by our culture and what society tells us to do. There are lots of "shoulds" and "should nots." Even if we free ourselves a little bit by doing our own thing, sometimes we may still re-play some old programs of what we should or shouldn't do.

Because of that, we may end up sacrificing our heart's desires and what we truly want. Then, we never feel good enough, we always expect obstacles, and they always appear. Then we complain or give up. The negative pattern may even turn into conviction and a negative cycle. This is such a heavy weight to carry! Eventually, we can become a master of creating things that are not good for us (but hey, since everyone is doing them, we should too, right? Otherwise, we may not get accepted).

The mind follows what everyone else is doing or what is considered prestigious. But is it good for you and your journey? I can't tell you, but your heart indeed can, and now you can practice tuning in. As with everything, it may take a little practice, but trust me, it will be worth it!

Remember, if you choose your own path and know it's your own unique path, why would you compare yourself to others and their unique path? It wouldn't make any sense.

Another example: Let's say your favorite color is blue, and you always dress in blue, as it makes you feel happy and aligned. At the same time, you don't really like green. Then you see everyone wearing green pants, and telling you it made them very successful. What would you do? Would you compare yourself to them and try to wear green just to fit in - even if it's not your color? Of course not. This is an extreme example, and some people may even say it's stupid. Unfortunately, this is the type of trick that our minds love playing on us.

When Abundance Doesn't Follow Confidence

Focus on what you have and what you truly desire without putting it on a pedestal and comparing yourself to others.

Most people focus on what they don't have right now. Even if everything is going well and they are attracting abundance, health, and happiness, they keep focusing on the fact that someone else is already a multimillionaire, has a super fit body, and lives in a better city. And yes, social media can really add to this constant comparison game.

This is why I advocate either quitting or drastically reducing your social media consumption or becoming more selective about what you consume. (As I'm writing this, I'm not on social media, and personally, I think it's lots of fun, but hey, different strokes for different folks. I'm just sharing what works for me!)

Realize your own unique journey and mission. Whenever your mind starts chattering and coming up with all those "but I should" thoughts and judgments, focus on your heart, feel its warmth...

Yes, you are the director and writer of your life, and your vision is up to you. But the Universe knows and understands the path of least resistance. Your self-image can work for you or against you.

Your attitude to anything that happens in your life determines how the next part of your journey will unfold.

When you get into this reactive state of mind, because you got attached to how much money you should be making, saving, attracting, and how other people should perceive you, don't react to it. Just observe it and let it go. Feel good about yourself just because you are, just because you exist, and just because you matter. You have nothing else to prove. You have already proven yourself by coming to this world.

Also, people who really feel good about themselves don't feel the need to feel guilty, justify themselves, or resort to being arrogant or cocky (another side of the spectrum) to hide their insecurities. Release the feelings of both inferiority and superiority. Replace them with neutrality and feeling of *I am enough*.

Just be! It's not that others must see you as this super confident person; it's about how you see yourself. It's about you giving yourself the permission to be you, authentically you. Play your own game. There's no

When Abundance Doesn't Follow Confidence

comparison to be made because no one else can play your game.

Chapter 7 - The Simple Mindset Shift Behind Unstoppable Motivation

Have you ever wondered why some people experience the constant need for external motivation and stimulation?

The truth is, if you know who you are, you don't seek motivation from other people to move forward because everything becomes automatic. You are your motivation. It comes from within you. It's ingrained in your self-image, so you don't really need to seek it from the outside world. And you don't need another dopamine hit just to keep going.

The old me, for example, had to watch dozens of motivational videos to get the motivation to write, maybe, two pages, but now I just get up early to write, and I write. It's normal for me. It's who I am. My thoughts, actions, and feelings: everything is aligned with my writing.

That is the power of clarity and giving yourself the permission to be you. This chapter will dive deeper into

The Simple Mindset Shift Behind Unstoppable Motivation

how to accomplish this by creating your life philosophy and mission.

You need to create your life philosophy; otherwise, you will become a master-servant of other people's philosophies or what motivates them (which may not be suitable for you and your own path in the long term). At the same time, it's also not about you repeating my life philosophy (I already said I don't want to indoctrinate my readers into my way of living and thinking).

You want to embody *your very own* life philosophy and live it. It will give you clarity and freedom, and you will no longer depend on others for your answers.

For example, my life philosophy is straightforward:

- *What do I do?*

- I help raise the vibration of the planet.

- *How do I do it?*

- I write.

- *Who do I write for?*

- I write for ambitious souls. People who understand the value of inner work and use it to manifest abundance

The Simple Mindset Shift Behind Unstoppable Motivation

(not only money but also inner peace and all the unique spiritual experiences) in all areas of their lives.

It took me a while to figure it out. But it doesn't have to be the same for you. I came up with a very simple exercise that works really well for most people who go through it. Some people may need a little bit more time, but it's still a significant, practical step to help them move forward and get more inner peace, focus, and clarity.

Exercise:

-Write down the names of people who genuinely inspire you and fuel your drive and ambition. The more you write, the better.

It can be someone you know in real life or someone you follow online or learn from. It can be a friend or a family member, or someone you don't know. As long as they inspire you in some way, write their names down.

Now, answer the following questions:

- What exactly inspires you in those people?

- How would you describe their life philosophy?

- What do they stand for, and what do they rebel against?

The Simple Mindset Shift Behind Unstoppable Motivation

- How do you feel about what they do or did and what they express about themselves?

Now tune into your emotions.

We are not trying to overthink the logic. Be true to yourself. There's no censorship here. Ask yourself:

- What emotions do you feel when you write about people who inspire you?

Here's the good news, you found those people impressive because the traits you admire in them are already inside you.

This is why you resonated with them, and they inspire you. Yes, it's pretty raw and may require some work. But at least you get some clarity as to what you want to represent.

So how would you use their most inspiring traits to describe your own life philosophy?

As you work through this process, try to limit the number of sentences and words you use. Can you finally pick just one word (or a few words) that describes your mission and your philosophy?

For me, personally, I would choose the word "vibration."

The Simple Mindset Shift Behind Unstoppable Motivation

Whenever I say the word: "vibration," it fills my heart with joy, and I immediately connect with my authentic motivation.

A friend of mine, for example, uses the word "expression." She's a dancer, and she teaches others too, so she sees her work as a tool to help people express who they are while eliminating resistance that holds them back.

A friend who is a yoga teacher uses "flow."

A person I know who is in sales uses the word "abundance," and another one says "money-honey" instead.

Don't be ashamed of your life philosophy and your mission. Practice redefining it and talking about it. Be authentically proud of who you are and what you stand for.

Of course, remember there is no hurry. Take all the time you need, and don't feel bad if you still don't understand your life philosophy. At least you are discovering it!

It will all come, and trust me, as soon as you have an idea and mission that is bigger and stronger than you, you will no longer struggle with motivation or confidence. It's like having your own muse, and the most significant victory you can have is to be faithful to and aligned with your own life philosophy. Your life philosophy will help you release your inner demons and everything that has been holding you back until now.

When you become what you desire and embody your desires, the rest will flow into your life. This includes the people, events, and circumstances that will help you reach your next level.

Think of it this way, your life mission and philosophy can help both you and others. Use it to create win-win scenarios.

One of the biggest manifestation killers is when you forget about your life philosophy and get distracted chasing other people's goals. This chapter is meant as a mental and energetic shield you can use to protect your authentic intentions for years to come.

Your Mission

Your philosophy is what drives you, but you also need your mission - an authentic and organized expression of you and something that can be measured as you do it.

The Simple Mindset Shift Behind Unstoppable Motivation

The best way to create your mission is to ask yourself what you want to accomplish in the next two to five years?

I have a five-year mission, and there is a certain amount of books on different topics (not just the LOA) I intend to write. I would also like to create a bigger team and get my books translated into other languages to reach more people (it goes back to my word- *vibration!*).

So, whenever some new shiny object presents itself, I just check in with my philosophy and my mission and ask myself – will it get me closer to or further away from what I desire to manifest? How does it feel?

My mission also motivates me to stay healthy. Whenever I say to myself, "vibration," I feel like eating more healthy fruits and veggies (high vibe foods).

Now, please note that a five-year mission may not be for everyone. If that's you, create a life mission just for the next year, or even the next month, just to test out this concept.

For example, a friend of mine has a simple mission for the next year - to record and upload 100 new videos to her YouTube channel, connected to her life philosophies

The Simple Mindset Shift Behind Unstoppable Motivation

of teaching, learning, educating, and inspiring. She loves learning about personal finance and testing different methods to make and save money, and then teaching an audience in her home country what she has learned via her YouTube channel.

So, whenever she sees an advertisement trying to distract her with some new business opportunity, she finds it easy to rest any temptations because she knows where her energy is better spent. After her mission is accomplished, she will look back at what she created and learn from it. She will focus on what worked, for example, what types of videos on her channel gained the most attention from her ideal audience and create another mission. It's all about keeping it simple!

One danger when it comes to accomplishing your mission is that you may feel tempted to neglect other areas of your life (which happened to me in the beginning). For example, you may want to speed up the process of your professional success by neglecting your health or family life. But remember - the Universe always seeks balance. And working with this law, staying in balance - even if it takes a little longer to accomplish your mission - will serve you much better in the long run.

The Simple Mindset Shift Behind Unstoppable Motivation

Also, remember, it's not about getting too obsessed with results. It's about the person you become as you go through fulfilling your personal or professional mission (or both). Like I said earlier, I will definitely work on expanding my team and getting some of my books translated into different languages.

However, I am not getting attached to goals such as, "I should sell this number of copies in this country. Otherwise, I am a failure."

Instead, I will choose the approach of mindful testing and curiosity. It will be fun to see how people in different cultures receive my ideas, so I will definitely learn a lot.

Even if your mission is so big it seems overwhelming, remember, it's not that you have to achieve a specific result as you go through it. It's all about enjoying your own game and your own process. Find as many little things you can learn from as you go through the process of fulfilling your mission.

Make it juicy and inspiring! Oh, and remember, you don't need to know all the steps. I still don't know all the steps and how to go through them. But I know they always unfold and come to me at the right time. I simply focus

The Simple Mindset Shift Behind Unstoppable Motivation

on the next word, the next sentence, the next page, chapter, and book.

The best mission is a mission that helps your personal goals while helping people on the other side. And yes, you can do it too. Go through this chapter as many times as you need to. Remember, if your role models inspire you in any way and you resonate with their goals and philosophies, it means it's also inside you! Isn't that thought alone motivating and inspiring enough?

Chapter 8 - Creating Your Own Unique Process to Manifest Desired Results

So you know who you are and what you want to attract. You know your life philosophy and mission.

Now you know what success means to you and how to integrate your authenticity into your daily actions to manifest your dream reality.

You have complete control over your body, mind, energy, and skills.

Success leaves clues, and success is a process.

Knowing and embodying are two different things. Your own process will be created by your own experiences and what works for you (you already know how to connect with your heart), plus what you may learn from others on a similar path (without comparing yourself to them, of course).

My daily process always consists of three simple, basic actions I can take today to effectively get closer to my mission. The small actions always compound over time.

Creating Your Own Unique Process to Manifest Desired Results

One of the actions I committed myself to is daily writing. This is the key to fulfilling my mission. A friend of mine who is a course creator and coach focuses on daily content through YouTube videos or doing Facebook Live streaming. Needless to say, copying her process wouldn't align with my mission and vice versa.

At the same time, your exact process is the key to manifesting your dream reality while becoming the person who attracts what they desire almost effortlessly.

Your process helps you develop the skillset you need to succeed with your desires. This will make you magnetic, and other people will perceive you as a leader, as someone who is grounded, unstoppable, and always gets what they want. People love positive action-takers as they motivate and inspire them!

You get to choose what you want to create in your life. Setting goals in contradiction with your self-image never works long-term. But now that you're getting in a full alignment, the way things will unfold will be truly magical.

As you truly embrace your own process, you refine and amplify your new, positive self-image.

Creating Your Own Unique Process to Manifest Desired Results

When I first got started on my journey, I was on a meager income and lived in a not-so-good neighborhood.

But I had a deep faith in myself and my process, and so it fueled my writing. I remember people telling me I couldn't do it, but since I was so immersed in my mission and my process, I knew that it was just a question of consistency, work, and focus in every cell of my body.

In my mind, my idea was that I was going to put one foot in front of the other and just keep going. Every day I looked myself in the mirror and congratulated myself on the steps I had taken. I kept calling myself a prolific writer. Even though I didn't have any substantial success to show initially, I quickly noticed that the way other people perceived and treated me began to shift pretty soon. I remember a family member who would always call me lazy and disorganized once called me out of the blue and said, "Wow, what you do is so inspiring! You are a writing machine! I think I'm gonna write my own book too!"

At that time, I also intuitively began doing mirror work, without even knowing what it was! I only researched it later when I was studying Louise Hay and her books. Just talking to myself kindly and looking at myself in the mirror and saying, "You are doing great!" helped me tremendously, as simple as it may seem.

It took me a while to figure out this simple formula:

Figure out who you are and what you really want.

Define it and be kind to yourself.

Fully believe in it and embody it.

Think and act as if you were that person already.

Do not expect approval, and don't seek it. Approve yourself and adjust your inner world accordingly.

Sooner or later, other people will start perceiving you as a leader, as someone magnetic, intelligent, and unique. In other words, whatever you created within yourself internally, and whatever friendly and kind words you told yourself (mirror work helps a lot in my humble opinion), those around you will sooner or later catch on.

I gave up seeking approval and validation, and I approved and validated myself. Eventually, my reality began reflecting my attitude, and even people who would constantly criticize me suddenly became kinder towards me.

Creating Your Own Unique Process to Manifest Desired Results

You can use the self-image formula in any area of your life. If you have a self-image of someone who enjoys eating healthy and exercising and see yourself as such, you will be successful on your health and weight loss journey, even before you get started on your new process.

Whatever goal you set for yourself, you can achieve, but first, make sure that your self-image supports your true authentic confidence and that everything is aligned.

Chapter 9 - Hidden Obstacles to Avoid (and the Real Truth about FOMO)

Whatever it is that you do, there will always be some temptations to resist. And even with your new self-image, self-confidence, process, and mission in place, you need to consciously protect yourself from the fear of missing out (FOMO). Because, the way our world works, there is always some temptation going on.

The truth is, the grass is not greener on the other side. The grass is always greener where your focus is. I see this happen all the time, in different industries, from forex to coaching.

Hmm... maybe you should give up your process and your mission because now everyone is doing this new thing, and you're missing out?

Of course, there are always some exceptions, and sometimes a good opportunity may present itself, and it will work perfectly well for you. Your heart will find the right answer for sure. But, if you tend to get distracted and fall off track all the time, then perhaps it's time to protect yourself from this negative pattern?

For example, right now, I'm really immersed in my writing process, and I have a schedule I'm very passionate about following. And only last week, an old friend contacted me with this new business opportunity that sounded very tempting because I already had a pretty decent skill set I could use to make it work. My friend told me several stories of people that succeed with his system and how I could easily do it based on my experience and skills. He said he could teach me the rest, and I'd pick it all up relatively quickly if I worked hard at it, and all he would need later would be my testimonial to help him promote his training.

Everything sounded great, and even the potential investments in marketing my new business weren't that big. It was a legitimate and pretty tempting opportunity.

For a few days, I felt an immense FOMO. But then, I asked myself, what kind of emotions would I get from any potential success in this new opportunity? A new community of entrepreneurs? A few new skills I could learn? That all sounds great, but there are also the emotions I can get just by focusing on doing what I do and doing it better and better.

If I chose to focus on this new opportunity, I would need to take a few months (or more) off writing. Not only that, but I would not be able to carry on my self-care routine and other projects that align with my big mission.

I kept diving deeper and asking myself:

If I was to accept his new opportunity, what would be my motivation? Would it be something positive or negative?

And I immediately realized that it was a negative, fear-based motivation (*I don't want to miss out on this!*) combined with fear (*Oh, but what happens when I lose my motivation and inspiration to write, perhaps I should do something else?*).

My mind was still trying to go against me again, with one more attempt: *Oh, but if this opportunity works out well, you can make more money which you can then use to turn more of your books into audiobooks much faster, expand your team, do translations into so many different languages, and you can hire more people to help you.*

Again, I had this fear of being too slow with my process and a feeling that I had to move faster and faster.

But then I re-connected with my life philosophy, my mission, and my process. Less is more. By focusing on one thing at a time, I can give it my full attention, which is the best thing to create my own steady pace. I can speed things up without trying to speed things up.

Embracing the process and getting into your authentic alignment is not always easy. And once we are there (like I am with my books), old patterns and temptations (including the fear of missing out on something new) may show up to tempt us. Remember, don't get seduced and stick to your path.

So eventually, I decided to pass on this new opportunity that a friend of mine was offering. I realized that there would always be many similar opportunities.

Also, when it comes to amazing opportunities that unleash your fear of missing out, why are they amazing? I mean, "amazing," for who?

I'd even venture to say that there is no such thing as "this new amazing opportunity." There's only this new amazing energy of yours, your focus, and what you decide to do with it. And your energy will make all your unique opportunities amazing!

The most effective way to get the breakthrough and manifest your deep desires is to stick with your process, even if some new temptation or old patterns crop up.

Hidden Obstacles to Avoid

Maybe it's the Universe testing you? Or perhaps it's your old self-image trying to squeeze in again and have its final word?

Whoever or whatever is behind it, you can use it to your own advantage to help you get even more rooted in your own process and follow it until your mission is finished and the chapter of your life that you're working on right now is closed.

Chapter 10 -Amplify Your Self-Image with Powerful Thoughts (What Most Gurus Don't Want You to Know)

Every thought you have carries specific energies. And it's your energy that determines the quality and outcomes of your actions. Your dominant thought is what determines your energy.

Your self-image is not just about the words you say and actions you take. It's also about your thoughts (and, therefore, your predominant energy).

The words you say stem from your predominant thoughts and your emotional patterns.

So, who are you at the thought and energetic level? Whatever you're thinking, you're also attracting. This is the basics of the Law of Attraction which I am aware most readers are familiar with.

So, how do you make your thoughts work for you? Is it possible to think 100% positive thoughts all the time? Or is there another option we can use to create the reality we want?

Amplify Your Self-Image with Powerful Thoughts

Well, it's not only about what we do, but how we do it. The way you think about what you desire is essential. And I'm not just referring to the simple "whether you think you can or cannot do it" kind of thought. We can dive even deeper than that. It's pretty obvious that if you think you can't do something, then the Universe knows you're not even interested, and so probably nothing will happen.

However, most people never consider this scenario (and most gurus never talk about it): you think you can do something, but you attach way too much importance to it, and you put it on the pedestal, which makes block your manifestations (the Universe always seeks balance). Be passionate about your goals, your life philosophy, and your mission, but don't fall in love with it. Find your balance.

Here's another scenario: you think you have positive thoughts or try to think positive, but deep inside, you still carry some limiting beliefs.

For example, let's say a person reads books on the topic of money and the LOA and tries to think positively. When asked about money, they just keep reciting the information they learned from books, saying, "Oh, money is good" and whatnot. Yes, they got the logical part, which is excellent. But then, deep inside, they may still fear money or feel sad about not having enough.

The best thing you can do is start with small baby steps to gradually change your feelings and emotions to develop the complete transformation and alignment. And you can do this by re-reading this book and aligning your self-image step-by-step.

Positive Repetition helps eliminate all kinds of negative blocks. It's as simple as that.

Whenever you catch yourself thinking your old thoughts, simply scan them and catch them. Don't judge them, and don't judge yourself for thinking them.

The best way to bring all your desires from the quantum field into the physical realm is to connect with them emotionally through your dominant thoughts. The more awareness you put on your thoughts, the easier this becomes.

Back to our previous example: a person reads a book about money and positivity and decides to use some affirmations such as, "I love money, I attract abundance," etc. When asked about money, they would tell you, "Oh yeah, I love it. Money is good!"

But then, they see someone who is successful, and they start judging that person and thinking thoughts such as: "Why are they carrying that expensive bag? Why do they tell everyone how much money they made or donated? And why do they spend their money on cars? If I were rich like them, I would do this and that..."

By the way, I used to be a bit judgmental, too: judging those who had money and those who didn't have it. You name it; I would always find a way to give them unsolicited tips about what they should do, haha.

I had to let it all go. I mean, who cares? Why keep judging other people? It's their life, their choices, and their energy. Everyone makes different choices. Some of my readers would love to buy expensive clothes, some would love to travel, and some would love to invest or donate. Some would love to do a bit of everything. People make different choices. Respect other people's ways, and you will attract more respect from others too. Once you have achieved that point, you will really feel like: *Wow, my predominant thoughts are positive, and my actions don't contradict them. Now, I can only attract more positive things into my life.*

Or perhaps you already know that feeling.

Accepting other people's choices without judging them is one of the most potent techniques to not only think positive thoughts but also to live by them and embody them.

Money wants to be your friend; true love wants to be your true friend; travel wants to be your true friend; whatever it is you want, also wants to be your friend.

Can you transform pain into power? Scarcity into abundance? Rejection into love? Whatever your old self did or attracted, you're safe now. Now, you're in a better place. Stay in this new vibration and watch your reality transform. I can't wait to see how it all unfolds for you!

Conclusion – Trust Yourself

Keep expanding and keep moving forward!

Watch your energy transform. Embody your desires. Be your desires. Affirm your desires with what you do and how you think about yourself, not only with what you say.

Don't get discouraged or impatient if it takes longer to manifest your desires; the journey itself is your destination. As you are exploring yourself and your manifestation abilities, you are becoming a better person. You are kind to yourself and others while cultivating a positive mindset infused with endless gratitude. That alone is a gift to those around you!

Keep practicing what you have learned, and keep sharing these concepts with others. Together we can change the world by collectively enhancing the vibration of the planet.

I genuinely hope that this book inspired you and gave you new tools to expand your consciousness and raise awareness.

You are limitless, you are powerful, and you are amazing!

Conclusion – Trust Yourself

I believe in you and wish you all the best on your journey!

If you have a few minutes, I'd really appreciate it if you could leave me a short review on Amazon. Let other LOA readers in our community know who this book can help, how, and why.

Thank You, Thank You, Thank You,
I hope we "meet" again,
Much love,

Elena

For more information and resources about LOA and manifestation, visit my website:

www.LOAforSuccess.com

If you'd like to say hi, please email me at:
elena@LOAforSuccess.com

Free LOA Newsletter

Join Our Manifestation Newsletter and Get a Free eBook

To help you AMPLIFY what you've learned in this book, I'd like to offer you a free copy of my LOA Workbook – a powerful, FREE 5-day program (eBook & audio) designed to help you raise your vibration while eliminating resistance and negativity.

To sign up for free, visit the link below now:
www.loaforsuccess.com/newsletter

Free LOA Newsletter

You'll also get free access to my highly acclaimed, uplifting LOA Newsletter.

Through this email newsletter, I regularly share all you need to know about the manifestation mindset and energy.

My newsletter alone helped hundreds of my readers manifest their own desires.

Plus, whenever I release a new book, you can get it at a deeply discounted price or even for free.

You can also start receiving my new audiobooks published on Audible at no cost!
To sign up for free, visit the link below now:

www.loaforsuccess.com/newsletter

I'd love to connect with you and stay in touch with you while helping you on your LOA journey!

If you happen to have any technical issues with your sign up, please email us at:

support@LOAforSuccess.com

More Books by Elena G.Rivers

Law of Attraction Short Reads Series

Money Mindset: Stop Manifesting What You Don't Want and Shift Your Subconscious Mind into Money & Abundance

How Not to Manifest: Manifestation Mistakes to Avoid and How to Finally Make LOA Work for You

More Books by Elena G.Rivers

Visualization Demystified: The Untold Secrets to Re-Program Your Subconscious Mind and Manifest Your Dream Reality in 5 Simple Steps

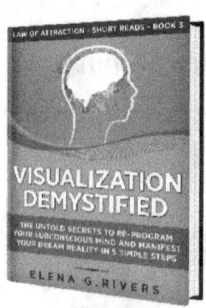

Law of Attr-Action for Entrepreneurs: Advanced Identity Shifting Secrets to Manifest the Income & Impact You Deserve

More Books by Elena G. Rivers

The Love of Attraction: Tested Secrets to Let Go of Fear-Based Mindsets, Activate LOA Faster, and Start Manifesting Your Desires!

Manifestation Secrets Demystified: Advanced Law of Attraction Techniques to Manifest Your Dream Reality by Changing Your Self-Image Forever

Script to Manifest: It's Time to Design & Attract Your Dream Life (Even if You Think it's Impossible Now)

www.ingramcontent.com/pod-product-compliance
Lightning Source LLC
Chambersburg PA
CBHW050505120526
44589CB00047B/2362